The Littlest Spoon

52 poems

by Jason Bates

Our Bed Should Have Been an Ark

It's all under water
now

A still-knotted tie
swims with black lace
panties, while our photographs
and technologies float off
down the hallway.

Last thoughts should not be
of shoes left in the middle
of the ocean floor,
nor of drowning
alone

Riding a Bicycle on a Gravel Road

I pull daisies from the raspberry scuffs

on your knees

and let them flutter off like wounded

butterflies

on the Indian Summer breeze.

You thank me by throwing

lithe arms around my neck

and asking for a carry

all the way back home.

I oblige,

but only for the kisses

I know will be customary

along the road.

Still Life

Our bed was the study
of contrasts.

Yours: a twisted mountain range
of tangled sheets and blankets
culminating at the tumultuous lake
of your mangled pillow.
The remains of dreams filled
with demons and desires.

Mine: the calm tropical ocean
of undulating bedding lightly
lapping the shore of the crater island
created where I laid my head.
My dreams paralyzed me.

Relationships

You cannot sing this song
without remembering
that time
when
we were alone
in your Father's
basement

On the green couch
that used to be
in your Mother's
livingroom

Honestly

I should have smiled
When you drew the curtains
Back and the morning
Sun instantly began to warm
Our bed.
I wasn't unhappy;
I just was not ready to face
The lie of another day.

While You Slept

I quietly tapped on your bedroom
window hoping that you might
understand and forgive me,
but only fools expect
such things while standing
on an overturned trash can
in the middle of the night.

Where the Remorse Goes

I carry my sorries in an old knapsack
wedged between a beaten up
copy of "The Red Badge of Courage"
and an unread edition of "Ordinary People".

I write my sorries on my arm,
my thigh,
my chest
before transferring them
into a small sketch pad.

I keep my sorries on shelves
scrawled on envelopes
and store receipts;
tucked inside the books
of mine that you never read.

The Words Inside Don't Matter

This journal has my initials
embossed in the upper
right hand corner
of the otherwise grey
faux-leather cover.

When you gave it to me,
you said that it reminded you
of elephant hide.

Now it just reminds me
of you.

Daffodils Do Not Weep for Orchids

We have all the same basic
Parts,
      You and I do.
We present different angles
      And curves,
But we make love the same way.

I am knight; you are princess.

I am Spring; you are new life.

I am me;
you are not better than that.

Autumn Age

The rake in hand is lighter
now than I remember it

The leaves less brightly colored

The pile is not the invitation
it once was

This man is no longer that boy

I Helped You Paint Your Walls

You erected your maze
of walls to protect
your heart from the intentions
of strangers,
but you left too much of your soul
in the colors that you chose.

re: hearse

Am I the only one
who,
in front of the mirror,
practices the eulogy
to be given at my
funeral?

The Preferred Method

Halos
are not intended
to be held up
by angelic hands

Arms grow tired
and it's impossible to sleep

Try, instead, to use
your horns
to hold that ring
above your head

Everyone Says I Look Like You

Some days, the first face I see
in the mirror is yours,
and the eyes that we share
cannot hide your disappointment.

This Morning

I drink my coffee, alone
and quiet, from a "World's Best
Dad" mug. I wrestle with the notion of smashing
it against the wall
for it tells one lie
over
and
over until I almost believe.

I do hope that my daughters
do not marry men like me.

Parenthetically Speaking

My mom added a dash
of love
to everything she cooked.

Me?
I do not stray from the recipe.

Trades We Should Not Have Made

ideals for responsibilities
wonder for fear
handlebars for better gas mileage
night stars for tv stars
truth for faith
experiences for comments
friendships for peers
cartoons for acronyms
dreams for memories

Last Night I...

Tossed and turned a lot.

Thought
random thoughts
like I should get a journal
to write down all these random thoughts, and I wish I
had some
molasses cookies like my mom
used to make, and if I get
a journal I should get
a nice pen, too,
and I don't
care
much
for the peel
and stick envelopes
—licking the adhesive is more
intimate…

Dragon

Ice falls from the sky
like a great dragon
laments the loss of her fire.

Three Things You Should Know About Me

i. On occasion,
the devil that lives
in my id
tries to strangle
the imp that resides
in my ego.

ii. I lie
awake
watching the drama
that we made
play out
on the empty
ceiling.

iii. Mine
is the sly
hand
that follows
the breeze
up
your skirt.

**There Are Many like It, but this Mental Illness is
Mine**

My left brain
and my right brain
dance the sixty-nine
but they both
use too much teeth

Triangles are Pointed like Horns

We make our own
Trinity—you
and me
and the man I used to be

A Fill in the Blank Poem

Things I Think About At Least Once a Day:

I should _____.
I should not _____.
I _____ a cigarette.
You are _____.
I _____ you.
I want to _____.
Look, a _____!

I'm the Most Terrific Liar...

My copy of The Catcher in the Rye is more special
than yours.

Yours has that red mess cover
of a wild carousel horse;
mine shows Holden from over
the shoulder, red hunting cap
on backward—there is a circle
worn from my index finger
pacing as I read.

Yours never addressed the term
"lonesome". You do not know
what it is like being
the lonely misanthrope.

Did yours ask you "Who wants
flowers when you're dead?"
And was the answer, like mine,
"Nobody"?

I grew up a thousand times
in one hundred eighty-nine pages;
yours is full of phonies.

Tea Time for a Kiss

You sip your tea
with the bag still steeping

paper tag dangling
beside the handle

Upon the last swallow
you press the bag
spent and warm
against your lips

That is not a kiss

Loaded

Sounds muffled like waves traveling through
Open wounds left by old knives
       and
Memories I kept locked and sharp
Under the remains of your
Cutest grins and poses
Hidden with the random thoughts
       and
Bodies of a thousand flamed out
Loves that you
Only heard about before
Ours
Died.

Smitten

Seeing your eyes staring at
Me, at the camera,
I could not stop
Tears from dropping puddles on
The photograph that
Even you must admit captures your
Natural beauty.

I Love You

Yes,
I have been drinking—

alone

while listening to every song
that could possibly
remind me
of you

and staring
into your eyes
in photographs—

Does that make it less
true?

On Flight and Song

Our lovebirds do not fly

or sing;

they only sit and stare

It's Not Gonna Put Mustard on Itself

Don't tell me
I'll like it if only I would
try it.
I've tried it,
and you do not know
how to love me.

Two Poems on The Lovers (two paintings by Rene Magritte)

1.
It was a beautiful day
in the hills

early Summer

a gentle breeze
provided some relief
from staining my suit

You were beautiful
and your plunging neckline
stole my heart

2.
We loved the Summer into
Autumn, days spent adventuring
evenings lingering embrace

we spoke
in hushed voice
of the time that you would leave

I'd hoped it would never
come
but tonight our kiss
is final

Before the Snows

If you were a snowflake
I'd catch you as you flutter
down a cold breeze
warning of an impending storm

I'd place you gently
in my jacket pocket
wrapped in a tissue
and nestle between cough drops and chapstick

I'd bring you inside
as you melt

Seal you in a bag
and store you in the freezer

Peppermint Does Not Taste Right With Cinnamon on My Lips

Last night
Autumn and I
lingered on the porch
prolonging the goodbye
with extra tears and sad kisses.
This morning I awoke
with Winter outside
my door asking
if she may
share my
bed.

Winter on the Coast

Take two steps
forward
into the awake-dream
of who you think
I am

Fall with me through
the cold sand
of a December
Massachusetts beach

Say your goodbyes
and settle your home
to bed
we are not to return
from the chill spray
and frothed foam.

Broken

Anyone who has loved
the first light flakes
of Winter snow
knows the heartbreak
of Spring's thaw.

Airplanes Do Not Sound like Trains

You

took me to

the airport so

we could watch the

planes take off. We spent the day talking about

everyday things like work and old friends who only

inhabit old

memories

and the last

time that

you made love to someone

who was

not

me.

But all I wanted was to listen to the trains echo

through the underpass near our old house.

Punk Marionette

Playing these punk songs
on your heart strings
is shredding my fingers
down
to bone and blood

But watching you flailing
in the pit
with tears in your eyes
and an X
on your hand
makes the pain worthwhile.

With "o" and "v" Left Over

I wake up every day
with letters rushing through
my bloodstream

Today they spell
"I love you"
Tomorrow could be
"You lie"

It's Like a Punch from a Small Fist

There is a specific kind of hurt
that penetrates the softest
area of the heart
when "I love you"
is followed by "I love you more."

Kiss Me Like Words Do Not Matter

You talk of good-bye
like there was some other
logical
conclusion
to hello

So Thick I Can Taste It

Your words are perfume

        h
     a
       n
      g
    i
      n
       g

in the   space   between us.

I Write Poems; You Write Death Threats

I sing punk songs with the birds
that have nested
outside your window

While you hold messages
up to the glass

But, honey, we both know
how far past
"I will call the cops"
we both are

I Should've Saved One, Unopened

I have opened

every

gift

you have to offer,

but I still

feel

empty.

Early Bird Misses the Moment

I dream about seeing dawn rise
through our bedroom window.
The sun lighting onto your closed
eyes and kissing those barely
parted lips.

I wake up too early, most days,
and my impatience gets the best
of me.

Impossible Math

"Your lips taste of chocolate,"
she said.

I did not register the compliment.

I was too distracted trying
to calculate how many days
we could fit into
our few short hours.

Breaking the Binding

I bent you over the arm
of the couch
like a new book

open, face down

to keep my place

Your:

eyes frame tear drops
like they were hand-crafted
for just that purpose

lips pout
as if sweet met sour
on the middle of your tongue
and you're unsure
which you prefer

dress lays just above
the knee
and cascades over the curves
along the way

innocence is scented
like wild flowers
on the first night
of Summer

Pollen

I bought her a bouquet of balloons

    different sizes and shapes

I doused them with flowery
perfumes stolen
from the department store counters

with a handmade card that read:
"I hope you're not allergic to latex, too."

We Do Not Need Music

You dance:

Like a smooth rolling tide
on high
from crest to break

Like a sine wave

Like you have just woken up from a long winter's
nap

Like the fox and the snake

Like pi

Like love is at stake

Like Newton was wrong about gravity

My Camera Broke; I Threw it Away

Lenses
and mirrors
capture the light
that reflects

Shutters
flutter at the sight

The aperture
dilates
attempting to capture
dreams

You

make

light

beautiful

Handwritten

As I whispered
toward
the door, I looked at you
sleeping
with your hip exposed
and for a moment
I wanted to write
words
on
you.

Twelve Short Poems to be Written on Her Body

1| You do not scare me, but loving you does.
  Terribly so.

2| May I stain my fingers with ink of varying colors;
  I can create a rainbow of your body?

3| I have forged my own key.
  Tell me please,
  fair Princess.
  Where does it go?

4| Your thighs are the warmest
  earmuffs
  I've ever worn.

5| You are beyond beautiful;
  This is my favorite curve.

6| You are not my type.
  My type is you.

7| I take no sugar in my morning
  coffee
  after kissing you goodbye.

8| Does the pen scratch? Do my
  words tickle?

9| My favorite part about writing
  this way is washing it off.

10| Our fingers, intertwined,
  are the first stanza.
  Our legs, entangled,
  the second.
  Our bodies, intermingled,
  the climax.

11| Fruits and sweets
      have more flavor
      when I use you as the plate.

12| I love you.

Made in the USA
Middletown, DE
28 November 2014